Curious Creatures

by Barry Louis Polisar

illustrated by David Clark

The Flying Paradise Snake of Borneo

Some snakes coil and rattle,
Slither, strike and hiss.
And now I've heard of everything:
Some fly; oh no, not this!

So I've unpacked my suitcase;
No trips to Borneo.
If snakes can fly between the trees,
Then I don't think I'll go.

Echidna

His nose is long and tapered,
He flicks his sticky spit.
His spiky tongue goes clicking
Wherever it will fit.

That tongue is two feet long,
Those gums smack back beneath.
He roots through plants to dine on ants
Because he has no teeth.

Beef

It's sad but true that beef is both
A full grown cow and meat;
I bet a cow would have a beef
With what some choose to eat.

The cow, I'm sure, prefers to graze
And happily grow fatter,
Eating grass or eating hay,
To lying on some platter.

Quokka

The quokka is a wallaby,
If that helps you at all.
A typical marsupial,
But curiously small.

The Earthworm

The earthworm lives beneath the soil
And spends life underground;
Too much sun and he is done for.
Too much rain and he will drown.
A gardener plants petunias
In a neat and pretty row;
The earthworm wiggles in the dirt,
Dodging spade and hoe.

The end can come at any time;
Bulldozed, dug up, cut in two,
A shovel's edge, a rake's sharp tine,
A tiller's blade, a hard-soled shoe.
A robin or a blue jay,
A starling or a crow
Can swoop down without warning
And pluck him from below.

Vultures

Vultures come in many forms
And many follow herds.
In fact, that's true of many things,
Not all of which are birds.

Be careful when within a crowd;
Watch what it is they follow,
How they act and where they go,
But mostly what they swallow.

Unau

The unau is a lazy sloth
Who lives life passively.
Like laundry on a clothesline,
He hangs down from a tree.

He sleeps most of the day away,
Though very few take note.
He moves so slow that mosses grow
And settle on his coat.

Dart Frog

He really is quite stunning
For such a tiny frog;
Sitting patiently alone,
Perched upon a log.

Brightly colored patterns
Run up and down his back.
His bumps contain a poison
Tucked in a tiny sac.

Though you might want to hold him,
You won't find him receptive;
Don't judge him by the way he looks
For looks can be deceptive.

Man

You know this guy. He's everywhere;
Uptown and 'round the block,
On the shoreline, in the woods,
On cliffs, in trees, on rocks.

He preys on other animals.
He's arrogant and brash.
He builds his home in every spot,
Then fills it all with trash.

The Fly

This pesky fly lands on my sandwich,
Hopping all around my plate.
Walking 'round my milk glass rim,
He dives below and tries to skate.

With darting jumps, he figure-eights,
Then stops to clean his face;
Leaves a trail upon my spoon
And germs on every space.

Lemmings

It's not true that lemmings
Commit suicide en masse,
As if they all were down and out,
Each in some deep morass.

Sure, the water takes them,
And though it's true they drown,
It's really overcrowding
That makes 'em all go down.

In searching for new habitat,
They'll gather on a ledge
'Til finally their numbers swell
And push them off the edge.

Ibex

Without a net or hiking boots,
Pulleys, cleats, or rope,
The ibex stands upon a ledge,
Balanced on a slope.

He'll butt his head against a foe,
Lock horns, then start to shove;
A thing that one should never do
In a place so high above.

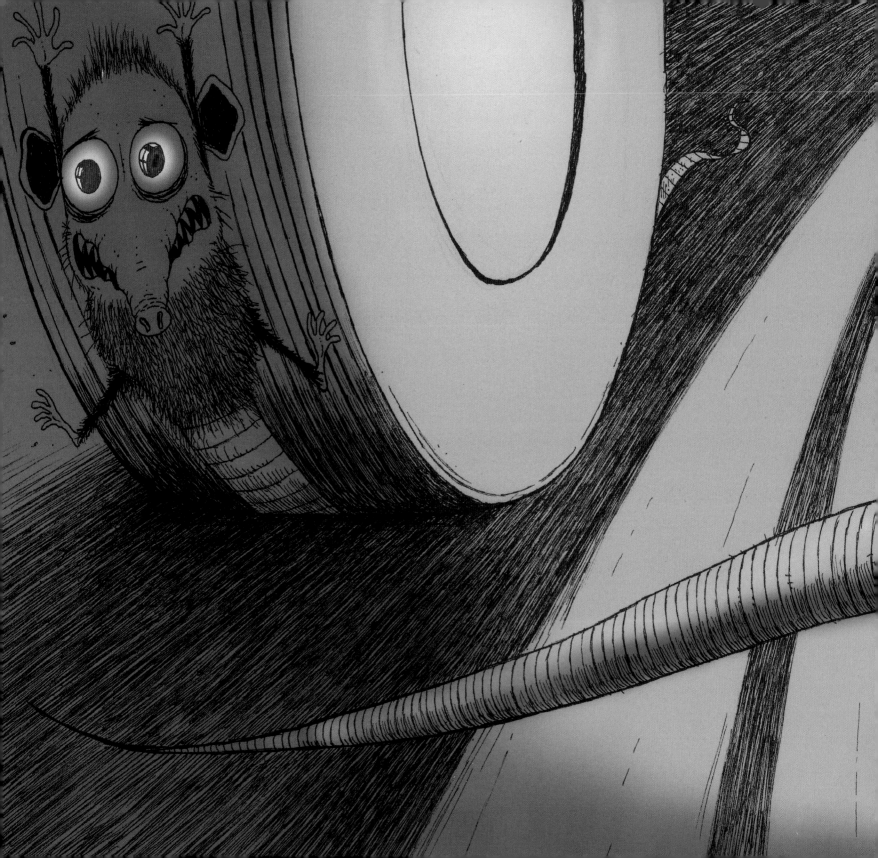

Opossum

Oh, poor, poor opossum,
Where do you go at night?
Why must you waddle in the dark?
Can't it wait 'til light?

Didn't mother tell you
That to live another day,
Before you cross a busy street,
You first must look each way?

Vicuña

Vicuñas from the Andes
Are related to the llama;
They're kinda like a camel
With a bit more melodrama.

If one of them gets angry
He'll show a lot of grit,
And like some children that I know
Will kick and hiss and spit.

They push and shove and carry on,
It really is so sad;
Their fur is neat and silky but
Their manners are so bad.

Bush Pig

You will not catch a bush pig dancing;
A bush pig works with what it's got.
It roots about with claws and snout,
But won't be something that it's not.

Flying Snakes of Borneo: These snakes don't really fly. They get their name because they flatten their bodies and glide between trees, which makes them look as if they are flying.

Echidna: Although they are sometimes called spiny anteaters and their diet consists largely of ants and termites, echidnas are not related to the anteater species. Native to New Guinea and Australia, echidnas are covered with coarse hair and spines and have long, slender snouts and small, toothless mouths. They feed by tearing open soft logs and anthills, using their long, sticky tongues to collect their prey.

Beef: One of the common names for cattle, beef is also the name for meat that comes from cows.

Quokka: Like kangaroos, wallabies and other marsupials, the quokka is a vegetarian. It is a nocturnal animal found on the islands off the coast of Western Australia.

Earthworm: To avoid drowning, earthworms often come above ground after a rainstorm, but can become stranded there and die from exposure to the sun, or be preyed upon by birds, snakes and mammals. Earthworms aerate the ground and play a major role in converting dead leaves into rich soil. Some species are able to regenerate lost segments after being cut in two, depending on the extent of their injuries.

Vultures: These scavenging birds feed mostly on the carcasses of dead animals and usually travel in groups. Most have a good sense of smell, and are able to detect dead and decaying animals from great heights. Vultures seldom attack healthy animals, but may kill the wounded or sick.

Unau: Also known as two-toed sloths, unaus will spend most of their lives hanging from trees. They are generally nocturnal animals and eat fruits, nuts, berries and bark. The food they eat can take up to a month to digest due to their slow metabolism. These exotic creatures even give birth while hanging upside down.

Dart Frog: Native to Central and South America, these frogs are generally found in tropical rainforests. Called "dart frogs" due to native people's use of their toxic secretions to poison the tips of blow darts, most poison dart frogs are brightly colored, displaying patterns to warn away potential predators. They secrete toxins through their skin and, as a result, are able to be active alongside potential predators during the day. Captive-bred animals do not contain significant levels of toxins. These frogs have been affected by the worldwide decline in habitat due to logging, farming and development.

Man: Humans are rumored to have a highly developed brain, capable of reasoning, language and problem solving. Their ability to make far greater use of tools than any other species, and to adapt to virtually all climates, has had a dramatic effect on the environment. Human activity has contributed to the extinction of numerous species of other creatures.

The Fly: The housefly is the most common of all flies seen in homes. They can hang upside-down from ceilings and walk vertically on walls. When they are not flying, flies continually clean themselves, rubbing their eyes with their forelegs and dusting off their legs by rubbing them together. Most of their taste and smell receptors lie on the hair of their legs. Because of how much they eat, flies deposit feces constantly, a habit which makes them unpopular houseguests.

Lemmings: It is a myth that lemmings commit suicide by drowning themselves in water, but the myth does have some basis in truth. Lemmings are self-destructive in that they reproduce so quickly that they soon run out of space. In their search for new habitat, they travel together in large hordes and once they pick a direction to travel in, they do not like to change course. When they encounter a body of water, they congregate beside it until their numbers swell so large that they have no choice but to jump in. As they swim, many do not make it to shore.

Ibex: These wild mountain goats are distinguished by the male's large, curved horns. Adult males have long, pointed beards and the species prefers to inhabit rugged terrain as a protection against predators.

Opossum: When threatened, opossums will mimic the appearance and smell of a dead animal. Also called possums, they eat insects, frogs, birds, snakes, small mammals and earthworms. Their diet mainly consists of carrion and many are killed on the highway while scavenging for road kill.

Vicuña: Relatives of the llama, these animals produce extremely fine wool. Vicuñas are very shy animals and are easily startled by intruders.

Bush Pig: Not to be confused with warthogs, bush pigs live in thick forests and are seldom seen during the day. They eat mostly roots and vegetable crops, and grunt while foraging for food.

Curious Creatures © 2010 by Barry Louis Polisar   Illustrations © by David Clark
Dedicated to Cousin Shelby 1935-2008
Published by Rainbow Morning Music 2121 Fairland Road, Silver Spring, Maryland 20904
ISBN # 0-938663-52-6
First Edition 2010, Printed in the United States of America